AMERICAN
COUNTRY
CHURCHES

A Pictorial History

JILL CARAVAN

COURAGE
BOOKS
AN IMPRINT OF RUNNING PRESS
PHILADELPHIA • LONDON

9 8 7 6 5 4 3 2 1
Digit on the right indicates the number of this printing

Library of Congress Cataloging-in-Publication
Number 96-69268

ISBN 1-56138-789-4

This book was designed and produced by
Todtri Productions Limited
P.O. Box 572, New York, NY 10116-0572

Author: Jill Caravan
Captions: Linda Greer

Publisher: Robert M. Tod
Editorial Director: Elizabeth Loonan
Book Designer: Mark Weinberg
Production Coordinator: Heather Weigel
Senior Editor: Edward Douglas
Project Editor: Cynthia Sternau
Associate Editor: Linda Greer
Picture Researcher: Laura Wyss
Typesetting: Command-O, NYC

Printed and bound in Singapore

Published by Courage Books,
an imprint of
Running Press Book Publishers
125 South Twenty-second Street
Philadelphia, PA 19103-4399

PICTURE CREDITS

CONTENTS

INTRODUCTION

$\mathbf{A}$top a hill, along a rural road I have traveled since childhood, sit the remains of a little country church. It was not the one my family attended, but I remember it well from having been there with friends.

The interior was plain but not stark, with wooden pews, a pulpit for the preacher, and space for a large choir. The four paned windows along each side are now boarded up, as are the double doors inside the portico in front. The building is grayish, not the starchy white of its livelier days. And the high tower above the sloping roof is now hollow without its welcoming bell.

A ranch fence still lines the dirt road leading up to the sunburned lawn, which doubled as a parking lot. Behind the building are a few headstones, all that remains of what was once a large church

RIGHT: Almost entirely lacking in external ornamentation, and with only a square belfry, this peaceful rural church is fairly plain compared with other churches of the same period. *Congregational Church, Acton, Maine; 1827.*

OPPOSITE: The octagonal spire of this Congregational church is interesting for its broad base, shingles, and touches of ornamentation. *Congregational Church, Manchester, Vermont.*

Built by a small group of pioneers, this non-denominational chapel, set in a magnificent, remote valley, is today a very popular spot for weddings. *Valley Church, Yosemite National Park, California; 1879.*

cemetery. To the side is a large, open, grassy area for picnics and other gatherings, shaded by a huge tree.

New housing developments now border the property on two sides, replacing farms whose families probably were members of the congregation. Across the road is a new super-highway. It gets much more traffic than the winding secondary road I use, a road that used to signal worshippers to slow their pace as they approached.

Usually, there is a fast-moving vehicle behind me as I near the hill. I always let the

other driver pass me so I can slow down to scan the building, lamenting the life that used to burst forth from its doors . . . when the pace of life was slower . . . when folks used to make it a priority each week to be together as a family and give thanks to their maker.

Many of us may recall a similar, idealized image of a country church. In reality, though, America's oldest places of worship are found in numerous shapes and sizes, represent many denominations and architectural styles, and have fascinating and unique histories.

The first settlers to descend upon the New World with church building in mind were the Spanish missionaries. Their goal was not to escape from the religious beliefs in their native land, but to spread those beliefs, to "save" the souls of the Native Americans in the new land. When the missionaries built their churches they held nothing back: They constructed substantial, ornate fortresses, intended to establish a presence and to astonish.

The Puritans, on the other hand, did come to the New World to escape religious persecution. They left behind the Gothic architecture of the church they had abandoned; their houses of worship were simple and serviceable, their communities built around them.

Virginia's settlers came to America to make their fortunes, so their churches were not generally the main focus of their communities. Instead, they erected "crossroads" churches—usually at convenient intersections—in proximity to everyone, but central to no one.

The one element all the denominations that eventually established themselves in the New World had in common was the desire for freedom to pursue their religious ideals. For a time, however, Protestantism came to overshadow the rest of the churches, from the period of the first Protestant settlement at Jamestown, Virginia in the early 1600s, until after the American Revolution and the founding of the country in the late 1700s. The only exceptions were Maryland (Catholic), Florida (New Spain), and the Northwest and Canada (New France). The Protestant majority attempted to make their church the law of the land—the very practice they had protested against by leaving

their homelands. This, naturally, caused a great deal of disharmony among the various religious, ethnic, and racial groups in the country, and even cost some people their lives.

Over the years, though, different areas of the country began to provide for religious liberty. Congregations that had not been permitted to worship legally won the right to proclaim their beliefs to the world. And, finally, in 1789, religious freedom in the United States was guaranteed by the First Amendment to the Constitution.

For some, however, the struggle has still not ended. Over the two hundred years since the Bill of Rights was enacted, there has been continued discrimination, and violence. As a result, some churches have been destroyed or abandoned. But today a great deal of American history is evident from within the walls of many of America's country churches.

FOLLOWING PAGE:
The nave of St. Francis Basilica contains a rear entrance and a graceful arcade flanking the center aisle, both serving to focus attention on the altar. *St. Francis Basilica, Dyersville, Iowa.*

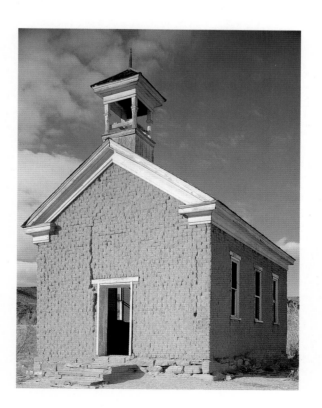

Long abandoned, this brick church in the ghost town of Grafton, Utah, like the adventuresome pioneers of the Old West who built it, is sturdy, straightforward, and functional. *Grafton, Utah.*

CHAPTER ONE

CHURCH ARCHITECTURE AND DESIGN

The word "church" is derived from the Greek *kyriakon doma*, meaning the Lord's House. The first Christians generally gathered in people's homes (and, sometimes, in catacombs). Because their services frequently involved a meal as part of the ritual, they often met in a dining room. At that time, dining rooms usually took up the entire top floor of the home, thus the term "upper room," also referred to in the New Testament: "And when they had entered, they went up to the upper room, where they were staying" (Acts 1:13); "And he will show you a large upper room furnished and ready, there prepared for us" (Mark 14:15).

THE FIRST CHURCHES

Originally the gathering room for worship was furnished with a table and three couches. But the Christian community was in the process of evolving, and by the third century, the room was furnished with a mensa, a special altar for the Eucharist. An armchair, known as a *cathedra*, was provided nearby for the presiding bishop. The word "cathedral"—a large church presided over by a bishop—is derived from the name of this seat.

Because of the evangelization of more and more Christians, the assemblies probably moved out of homes and into other public places. Unfortunately, there is no written record of this; the early Christians kept their places of worship secret to avoid persecution.

Eventually Christianity was recognized by the Roman emperor Constantine the Great, who accepted the new religion as his own faith in A.D.

312 before he went into battle against his rival, Maxentius. Ultimately Christianity became the official religion of the Roman state, and even today the Vatican in Rome is the seat of the Roman Catholic church, which claims apostolic succession from the original church.

THE CRUCIFORM PLAN

It was during the fourth century, after the enactment of the Edict of Milan in A.D. 313, that the

OPPOSITE: This typically plain eighteenth-century meetinghouse has an unusual nineteenth-century tower and steeple, thought to have replaced an original porch. *Old Meetinghouse, Jaffrey, New Hampshire; 1775.*

BELOW: Erected by an Acadian community, Lille Cathedral exhibits many of the elements of the cruciform plan, including a raised sanctuary containing an altar, and clerestory windows above the center aisle. Today the building is used as a community center. *Lille Cathedral, Lille, Maine; 1909.*

This well-proportioned steeple exhibits many of the elements popular in the nineteenth century: a square tower with a clock and open belfry, decorative moldings and columns, and an octagonal spire. *First Congregational Church, Lee, Massachusetts.*

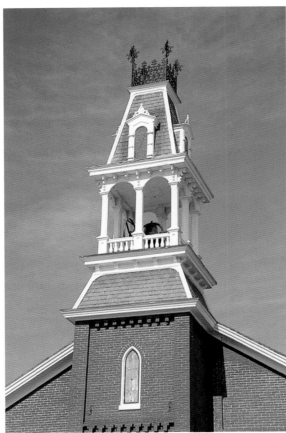

A large bell in an open-arched belfry is the dominant element in the entrance tower of this Lutheran church. The wrought-iron railing surmounting the roof suggests a medieval lookout post. *St. Marks Evangelical Lutheran Church, West Fairview, Pennsylvania; 1869.*

church emerged from underground and the first buildings known publicly as "churches" were built. These buildings were separate from homes; once the religion became a part of the state, the Christian liturgy took on a more regal, dignified style.

Constantine's architects were inspired by the Roman basilica, which was then a large, public hall used mainly as a court of law. The early Christian basilica was a longitudinal building with some or all of the following architectural elements:

> **Nave**: the central portion of the building, extending from the entrance of the central room to its front, flanked by side aisles.
>
> **Arcade**: a series of arches with columns or piers.
>
> **Clerestory**: a row of windows above the aisle in the nave.
>
> **Apse**: a semicircular area at the front of the nave where the clergy sat. Clergymen replaced the magistrates of the courts in the apse, which was separated from the congregation by a screen or railing. This barrier was a forerunner of the Communion rail, which communicants approached to receive the Eucharist. The clergy were even more separated from the laity in Byzantine churches.
>
> **Transept**: a transverse aisle across the front of the church separating the nave from the apse.
>
> **Altar**: the main table of the Lord, the focus of the sanctuary and entire church. It stands by itself so that the ministers can move about it freely, and is situated so the ministers face the congregation.
>
> **Sanctuary**: the part of the church where the altar of sacrifice is located and where the ministers lead the people in prayer, proclaim the Word of God, and celebrate the Eucharist. It is set off from the body of the church by a structural feature (such as elevation above the main floor) or by ornamentation. The sanctuary is located at the front or center of the church.

The basilica design—with a central nave, aisles down the sides, and an apse at the end—is known as the cruciform plan. It displays great reverence, as the longitudinal layout places the worshiper entering the church in a direct line of sight to the sanctuary in the apse. This is reinforced by aisle columns which further focus attention on the altar. Many basilicas were even built on an east–west axis, with an altar at the east end facing Jerusalem.

TOWERS AND SPIRES

Early churches were topped not only by domes, but also by towers—square, flat-roofed structures higher than their diameter. A spire—a tapering roof surmounting the tower—was added to some churches as well. (The term "steeple," often used interchangeably with "spire," refers specifically to a graduated type of spire which sometimes resembles a crown.) During medieval times, the towers and spires on churches in Europe grew to new heights and became increasingly ornamented.

As cities developed around churches, the towers and spires were used as landmarks, helping people to locate their house of worship from a distance. At a time when there were few houses more than two stories tall, churches and cathedrals towered over the rest of the buildings, giving identity to the community. These soaring structures were seen as religious symbols as well—to some as "a finger pointing heavenwards."

The first towers were also used as perches for watchmen on the lookout for oncoming trouble. Similarly, during the Revolutionary and Civil wars, American church towers often served double-duty as strategic landmarks or sighting posts. Some have even served as navigational aids for ships plying nearby waters.

Many church towers house a bell or several bells and, sometimes, provide space for bell ringers. The section of the tower that holds the bell is called a "belfry"; if the entire tower is devoted to the bell, it is also termed a belfry, or bell tower. Clocks, too, are commonly incorporated into one or more sides of towers. Both bells and clocks serve to remind parishioners when the time for worship has arrived.

Often the most ornamental parts of church exteriors, towers, spires, steeples, and belfries in America, particularly in the East, were frequently patterned after English designs. Beginning in the

Architect Lavius Fillmore (a cousin of President Millard Fillmore) introduced a new type of steeple when he designed this Vermont church. The belfry, with its high, open arches, is particularly graceful. *Congregational Church, Old Bennington, Vermont; 1805.*

mid-eighteenth century, with the increasing English influence on American fashions, many denominations erected elaborate structures atop their churches, often with several graduated stages (including a belfry), windows, arches, columns, pilasters, and other decorative elements.

PULPITS AND PEWS

In medieval times, congregations stood or knelt during mass; only the choir and clergy had stalls, enclosed spaces with fixed seating reserved for their use. During the Protestant Reformation in the sixteenth century, the emphasis shifted away from the mass and toward preaching, so seating was needed for the attendees. Benches, at first with no backs, and box pews were introduced, and eventually required more room in the church to accommodate them.

In some churches, pews were arranged down the sides, and in others, they filled the middle. As congregations grew, "hanging pews" or galleries were added to accommodate more people along the sides, toward the back, and in the corners on either side of the Communion table.

Pews were assigned in some churches—the frontmost and the largest to those families considered most important—and marked to reserve them. In colonial America some families purchased pews for their exclusive use.

These extremely simple, white pews are typical of New England's early meetinghouses. Large, clear windows allowed parishioners to read their hymnals and prayer books without artificial lighting. *First Congregational Church, East Machias, Maine; 1836.*

RIGHT: Plain, open white pews in this 1819 church contribute to the airiness of the interior. The gallery (hanging pews) was added around 1858. *St. Thomas and St. Denis Episcopal Church, Cainhoy, South Carolina; 1819.*

OPPOSITE: The simplest of towers, with its traditional weathervane, serves as belfry and entrance for a coastal Maine church. *Saunders Memorial Church, Penobscot Bay Peninsula, Maine.*

With the Protestant emphasis on preaching, the altar was replaced by a pulpit, or ambo, a lectern at which the minister stands. Toward the end of the sixteenth century, new designs moved the pulpit to the side of the church. This repositioning of the pulpit necessitated the rotating of the pews, which were then arranged to face the side pulpit; the main entrance door, behind them, opened in the middle of the long side. This arrangement can be seen in the "Old South" Church in Boston, built in 1729, and was typical of New England meeting-houses until well into the eighteenth century.

The Puritan denominations sometimes placed a sounding board above the pulpit, a disc that is the counterpart of the baroque *baldacchino* (embroidered canopy) above an altar. Congregationalists, on the other hand, built prominent, solid pulpits, but without elaborate decoration. Other Protestant denominations elevated the pulpit five or six feet, with steps leading up to it on one or more sides, or even a door, much like a courtroom witness stand. The Quakers, however, needed no pulpits (there is no preacher or minister in the Quaker tradition); they saw the elaborate, ornate pulpits of traditional Catholic and Anglican churches as overdone.

Sometime pulpits were built to accommodate more than one speaker. One denomination employed two pulpits; their sermons were similar to a dialogue between two speakers. Some churches provided for many members of the congregation to speak—rather than just one revered preacher—with groups of elevated pulpits, including tiers for various grades of presiding officers. Even with this emphasis on preaching, however, members were conscious of the length of the sermons, and at least one church is known to have installed a ninety-minute hourglass on the pulpit to limit the speaker.

ABOVE: **Though built in 1806, "Old White's" interior (and parts of its exterior) was remodeled in 1859. The small gallery at the rear is illuminated by unusual windows with a geometric motif. *Woodstock Congregational Church ("Old White"), Woodstock, Vermont; 1806.***

RIGHT: **The interior of St. Michael's Episcopal Church contains the original, raised pulpit with its massive sounding board, and a stunning Tiffany window depicting St. George slaying the dragon. *St. Michael's Episcopal Church, Charleston, South Carolina; 1752–61.***

OPPOSITE: **Rows of simple, varnished wooden pews provide a counterpoint to the intricately painted and beamed ceiling of this rustic Episcopal church. The pulpit is similarly plain, raised only a step above the nave. *St. Andrews Episcopal Church, Newcastle, Maine; 1883.***

WINDOWS

When one thinks of churches, the image of stained-glass windows automatically comes to mind. The Resurrection, the Birth of Christ, saints or scenes from the Bible, elaborate geometric patterns—these have all been highlighted in stained glass in churches throughout history.

The use of colored windows began in ninth-century Roman times, when thin, blown glass began to replace molded glass. The fine art of stained glass is believed to have been developed during the reign of Charlemagne along with the revival of such arts as enamelwork, which resembles early stained glass. Unfortunately, modern technology has yet to discover the secrets of the medieval techniques.

Stained glass, equated with divine light from heaven, was associated almost exclusively with church buildings from the late eleventh through the thirteenth centuries, part of the Gothic period. Prior to that, church art consisted only of murals or mosaics on large walls.

In addition to the side and front windows, stained glass was used in clerestory windows, above naves, in pediments, over doors and windows, and on building fronts. Windows also appeared in choir lofts, above altars, and wherever decoration was desired. The rose window, a large, circular stained-glass win-

dow, was another popular feature. Tracery, decorative openwork of stone or wood, was often used above the windows as an accent.

After the Reformation, some churches of the English Renaissance style were built with clear glass windows. These allowed more light into the church, making it possible for the congregation to follow along with the service in their prayer books. Also in contemporary Reformation churches, and later in mission churches in the southern and western United States, hidden windows were used to spotlight the altar.

RIGHT: **Echoing the shape of the vaulted ceiling, these tall, Gothic-inspired stained-glass windows illuminate and provide a focal point for this sanctuary.** *Church of the Holy Cross, Sumter, South Carolina; eighteenth century.*

OPPOSITE: **The beautiful windows of this New Hampshire church are further enhanced by the delicacy of their painted details.** *St. Patrick Church, Nashua, New Hampshire.*

LEFT: This large, pointed-arch window features a subtly colored, typically Gothic abstract flower and leaf motif. *Trinity Episcopal Church, Mackinac Island, Michigan.*

LEFT: Intricately detailed side windows in this gothic-style basilica may not provide a great deal of light, but they serve to remind parishioners of the "divine light of heaven." *St. Francis Basilica, Dyersville, Iowa.*

OPPOSITE: A praying Madonna is a common theme in pictorial windows; this one, with its richly colored stained glass, is reminiscent of those found in the medieval churches of Europe. *St. Patrick Church, Nashua, New Hampshire.*

The influence of English architecture on American church building can clearly be seen in this 1806 church, with its prominent portico and classical detailing. The entrance bay was deepened and the porte-cochère added in 1859. *Woodstock Congregational Church ("Old White"), Woodstock, Vermont; 1806.*

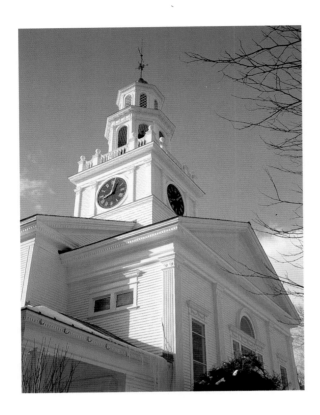

INFLUENTIAL ENGLISH ARCHITECTS

Sir Christopher Wren (1632–1723) was the most renowned English architect of his time. After an extensive fire destroyed much of the city in 1666, he was commissioned to rebuild more than fifty of London's churches. Wren chose to leave the heavy, Gothic style in the past, instead turning to classical architecture for his inspiration. He omitted the separate sanctuaries of his new churches, instead placing the altar at the end of the nave, thus lessening the impact of the altar and emphasizing the pulpit. He also designed lighter interiors with paler colors and clear glass windows, replacing the dark colors and stained glass of the medieval churches. Wren added an innovative variety of towers and steeples to his churches as well. Although they were not seen to have any real significance at the time, these changes may have foretold what was to come in the midst of the Protestant Reformation.

James Gibbs (1682–1754) was considered the most important London architect of the eighteenth century; many architects, both European and American, were influenced by his designs, which were widely circulated in books. Gibbs, in turn, was influenced by the work of Christopher Wren. A native of Scotland, he went to Rome to study for the priesthood, but instead studied painting and architecture under Italian architect Carlo Fontanas. Gibbs' unique style combined both Italian and English forms. St. Martin-in-the-Fields, with its Gothic steeple and classic portico, is his best-known work, and was much imitated in American church architecture.

From 1760 to 1780, England's largest architectural firm was owned by the three Adam brothers; the oldest, Robert Adam, is considered the most talented and innovative. The Adam style, also called the Federal style in the United States, reached America by 1775. Like the earlier Wren and Gibbs designs, Adam buildings incorporated numerous classical elements. In the Adam style, however, these motifs received a lighter, more delicate treatment: Columns and pilasters were narrower and more widely spaced, moldings and ornaments were in lower relief, and curves and arches were used more frequently.

POPULAR ARCHITECTURAL STYLES IN THE EAST

Wren, Gibbs, and the Adam brothers were all masters of the architectural style broadly referred to as "Georgian" or "Porch and Portico." The work of these architects represents three major branches of the style; the only unifying theme of Georgian architecture is its reliance on classical forms. Details within the style differ greatly, becoming more refined toward the later years of the period, which lasted from 1714 to about 1830 in England.

The Georgian style exerted its influence on American ecclesiastical architecture for many years, reaching its height in the second half of the eighteenth century. Remaining examples of Georgian churches are particularly numerous in the eastern states, where Anglicanism was

OPPOSITE: Gothic Revival details such as pointed-arch windows figure prominently in the design of this small, charming Connecticut church. *St. Bridget Church, Cornwall Bridge, Connecticut.*

ABOVE: Demonstrating the versatility of the style, a small sect known as Swedenborgians erected this solid, archetypical Greek Revival church on the Maine coast in 1843. *The Church of the New Jerusalem (Swedenborgian), Bath, Maine; 1843.*

RIGHT: The Gothic Revival style received a relatively light treatment on the exterior of this Congregational church. The verticality of the tower is reinforced by the use of small spires as decorative elements. *Winter Street Church (Congregational), Bath, Maine; 1843.*

widespread and congregations were wealthy enough to afford these relatively elaborate structures. While the grandest Georgian churches were designed using the cruciform plan, usually following the examples of Wren and Gibbs, many simpler churches also displayed typical Georgian ornamentation. After the Revolutionary War, however, most denominations that had previously favored the plain meetinghouse form (except the Quakers) turned to the basilica as well.

The Classical Revival developed as a further refinement of the Georgian style; the Adam style was a transition between the two. Unlike the earlier English-inspired Georgian architecture, however, the Classical Revival was mainly an American movement of the populous and wealthy Northeast and Mid-Atlantic. The period began after the Revolutionary War and continued into the first half of the nineteenth century, when it spread to the Midwest.

The most highly developed Classical Revival, or Neoclassical, churches were generally built by Congregational and Episcopal groups. They are distinguished by their ornate, colonnaded porticoes and extremely tall, detailed, multi-stage towers and spires. Simpler Neoclassic churches, built by more conservative or less wealthy denominations, have less ornamentation, and frequently include an entrance tower rather than a roof tower and portico.

During the middle part of the nineteenth century, roughly from 1825 to 1860, America experienced a church-building boom. One style, Greek Revival, became extremely popular because of its versatility and suitability to any denomination. Based on ancient Greek temple designs, the style is typified by comparatively plain, rectangular buildings, often without a projecting porch or tower, but invariably including columns. The naves of Greek Revival churches also tend to be wider and shallower than those of Georgian or Neoclassical churches, bringing the congregation in closer contact with the pulpit.

Another revival movement, the Gothic Revival, began around 1840 and lasted until just after the Civil War. This style grew out of a reaction

The small vestry at the rear of this simplest of Georgian churches is the only remaining part of the original structure, which burned in 1815; the new building was completed in 1819. Some of the gravestones in the churchyard date to 1782. *St. Thomas and St. Denis Episcopal Church, Cainhoy, South Carolina; 1819.*

Pointed arches and heavy, wooden doors, typical of the Gothic Revival style, adorn this rural New Hampshire church. *New Hampshire.*

against the Greek Revival; some considered the older style to be a pagan form, and desired a return to the more "Christian" architecture of the middle ages. It was particularly popular among Episcopal and Catholic parishes, and was spurred by another Englishman, A. W. Pugin.

Typical elements of a Gothic Revival church include pointed-arch doors and windows, a square tower with a belfry, and quatrefoil devices. Often of stone or board-and-batten construction, these buildings tend to be rather irregular in shape, with additions such as a baptistry, transept, or vestry projecting out from the nave.

WESTERN ARCHITECTURAL STYLES

In the Southwest and California, where Catholicism dominated into the early nineteenth century, two styles of church were prevalent: Pueblo and Spanish Colonial. The older Pueblo style, found mainly in New Mexico, was executed using building techniques adapted from those of the indigenous Pueblo peoples. Nearly windowless, flat-roofed, thick-walled structures of sun-dried adobe, Pueblo churches were sometimes embellished with a few Baroque details, but generally remained fairly plain on the exterior. Inside, however, the simple naves and sanctuaries often contained richly painted murals and panels which incorporated Indian motifs into the Christian iconography.

The Spanish Colonial churches, which include all of the Franciscan missions in California, Texas, and Arizona, were elaborate structures replete with Spanish and Mexican Baroque ornamentation. This type of decoration was typified by a profusion of carving and scrollwork (particularly surrounding the entrance), pilasters, colorful artwork, and niches containing statuary. Most Spanish Colonial churches also have one or—more commonly—two belfries, and sometimes include one or more domes and a vaulted roof.

Constructed of adobe or stucco-covered limestone, these churches were fully developed examples of the cruciform plan, but were only one part of a large complex of buildings—including housing and work spaces—surrounding an interior courtyard. Many missions had a spacious plaza outside the front of the church, as well. Unfortunately, most of the missions fell into disuse by the 1820s, and the remaining ones were not restored until the first half of the twentieth century, during a resurgence of interest in local architecture.

RIGHT: **The Serra Chapel contains a spectacular gilded screen and pulpit, both examples of the Spanish Colonial style at its most ornate. The niches with statues and the painted details are also typical.** *Mission San Juan Capistrano, San Juan Capistrano, California; 1776 (church); 1777 (Serra Chapel).*

OPPOSITE: **Although the walls of this Pueblo-style church in the Sangre de Christo Mountains were built using some of the Indians' techniques, the wooden beams, doors, and decorative elements are purely Spanish additions.** *Mission San José de Garcia, Las Trampas, New Mexico; mid-eighteenth century.*

ABOVE: One of the most elaborate of the Spanish
Colonial missions, San Xavier del Bac boasts intricately
carved decoration both outside and in. The mission
was founded in 1697 by a Jesuit, Father Eusebio Kiño.
Mission San Xavier del Bac, Tucson, Arizona; 1767–97.

OPPOSITE: Set in adobe-covered tufa (limestone)—the most
favored construction material among the Texas missions—this
window, with its curves and carvings, is representative of the
baroque Spanish style. *Mission San José, San Antonio, Texas.*

CHAPTER TWO

HISTORIC CHURCHES AND CHAPELS: NEW ENGLAND, THE MID-ATLANTIC, AND THE MIDWEST

The first structures used as houses of worship for the English settlers in the New World were built on Roanoke Island in what was the territory of Virginia, and at Sagadahoc on the Kennebee River in what is now Maine. Simple buildings of log construction, they were not intended to be permanent, so they have not survived. Fortunately, a great many other church buildings erected on our shores have survived; what follows is a brief tour of some of the most historic church buildings that remain, and an explanation of the religious movements that inspired and influenced their architecture.

THE PURITANS

Puritans in the sixteenth century held the conviction that the church should focus on fellowship and be restored to simplicity and purity, as it was in the first century. Although there were some reforms after the Anglicans broke off from the Roman Catholics, the Puritans felt that these had not gone far enough. They advocated spontaneous prayer, longer sermons, plainer vestments (without crosses), and no observance of Christmas. Both groups believed in the authority of the Bible, but the Anglicans did not take the Scriptures as literally as did the Puritans.

BELOW: The "Old Ship" is the only surviving example of an early, square Puritan meetinghouse. Ships carpenters may have built this unique structure; the loft's timbers resemble a ship's frame, and a painted compass adorns the ceiling under the cupola. *Hingham Unitarian Church ("Old Ship" Meetinghouse), Hingham, Massachusetts; 1681.*

OPPOSITE: Gothic doors and windows adorn this hilltop church in Nova Scotia. Small fleurs-de-lis atop the spire's dormer windows act as a quiet reminder of the French heritage of the area's early settlers. *Eglise Sacré-Coeur, Saulnierville, Nova Scotia.*

BELOW: "Old North" Church's steeple, which houses a peal of eight bells cast in England, was blown down by hurricanes twice in its history. After the first time, in 1804, it was rebuilt following the same design as the original, but sixteen feet shorter. *Christ Church ("Old North") (Episcopal), Boston, Massachusetts; 1723.*

The English Protestants who established themselves in New England—in Massachusetts and Connecticut—were all Puritans. Those who settled at Plymouth, Massachusetts—the Pilgrims—were separatists from the Church of England; they became known as Independents or Congregationalists, because of their belief that only local people should have authority over the church. They felt that God made a covenant directly with the people, not just with the church government. Ironically, after they came to the colonies to establish their own religious freedom, they used that freedom to reject those who differed from them.

HISTORIC PURITAN CHURCHES

Nineteen miles southeast of Boston, in Hingham, Massachusetts, is the "Old Ship" Meetinghouse, dating back to 1681. It is probably so named because its frame roof resembles an inverted ship's hull, and its belfry features a "lookout" station. It is a blend of Gothic as well as Puritan architecture, representing a break from the Church of England and intended as a simple gathering place. The structure was enlarged and remodeled in 1731, 1755, and 1930.

The three-level pulpit is the most spectacular feature—and the only remaining original part—of King's Chapel, Boston. Originally built in 1717, the church was the first in America to be officially governed by the Anglican Church in America (1787). It was also the first large granite building in the colonies. The interior of King's Chapel was based on St. Martin-in-the-Fields, designed by James Gibbs.

One of the proposed steeple designs from Gibbs' St. Martin-in-the-Fields, rising to a height of 185 feet, was used on the First Baptist Church in Providence, Rhode Island. This church, the oldest Baptist church in America, was founded in 1639 soon after Roger Williams and his followers settled, and was dedicated in 1775.

Like Gibbs', Christopher Wren's innovations were copied in many churches, including Christ Church in Boston—also known as the "Old North" Church—thought to have been designed by William Price. The steeple of this historic church, which was begun in 1723, was torn off by hurricanes in 1804 and again in the mid-twentieth century, but was replaced on both occasions.

Wren's designs also influenced the architects of St. Paul's Church—"Old Narragansett"—in Wickford, Rhode Island, the oldest Episcopal church in New England. Build in 1707 of oak and plaster, it was supported by the Society for the

RIGHT: Completely unique, the "Round Church" (actually sixteen-sided) was erected as a joint project by five different groups: Congregationalists, Baptists, Methodists, Universalists, and Christians. *"Round Church," Richmond, Vermont; 1812.*

OPPOSITE: Inside the belfry of this mid-nineteenth century Congregational church hangs an undoubtedly treasured bell, inscribed "Revere & Co. Boston 1817." *First Congregational Church, Topsfield, Massachusetts; 1843.*

RIGHT: An idyllic New England scene: a covered bridge, the changing colors of autumn, and a charming country church. The two doors may once have been separate entrances for men and women. *Stark, New Hampshire; seventeenth century.*

RIGHT: The great American poet Robert Frost is buried in the cemetery of this picturesque Vermont church. One can imagine the inspiration he must have derived from a winter scene such as this. *Bennington's Old First Church (Congregational), Bennington, Vermont; 1805.*

OPPOSITE: The well-kept cemetery adjoining the "Old Church on the Hill" holds the remains of numerous nineteenth-century parishioners, some of whose descendants still live in the area. *Community Church ("Old Church on the Hill"), Lenox, Massachusetts; 1805.*

Propagation of the Gospel in Foreign Parts (SPG) of London. It features a gabled roof and four Palladian windows on the long sides. St. Paul's was rebuilt and moved in 1799, and its original wineglass-shaped pulpit was replaced.

THE ANGLICANS

Unlike the Spanish and French missionaries, who came to spread their faith, the Anglicans, as well as the Puritans, came to America to escape the faith that had taken over England.

When Christopher Columbus landed on the shores of the New World, he left behind a Western Europe that was almost completely Catholic (except for a few pockets of Judaism). Just a generation later most of northern Europe defied the pope, and tried on Protestantism, a new form of the Christian faith.

England's Reformation occurred primarily because Henry VIII wanted male heirs, which his wife, Catherine of Aragon, could not give him. In order to obtain a divorce, he broke with the Roman Catholic church and established the Church of England. Although Henry remained a Catholic all his life, the break with papal authority was completed by the Act of Supremacy, which vested in the king all authority over the Church of England. Henry also provided his subjects with the first English translation of the Bible, and in 1549 the first Act of Uniformity was passed, making the new Book of Common Prayer the only legal prayer book.

When Elizabeth I became queen in 1558, she declared religious freedom, insisting, however, that her subjects attend services only of the national religion. Most of the people were Protestants in that they did attend Church of England services, and they accepted that there

BELOW: A soaring Gothic Revival Congregational church, quite a departure from the original, simple Congregational meetinghouse style, graces the Maine countryside.
First Congregational Church, East Machias, Maine; 1836.

ABOVE: The plain interior of First Congregational Church, with its large, clear windows and white walls and pews, stands in contrast to the more ornate facade (left).
First Congregational Church, East Machias, Maine; 1836.

OPPOSITE: Methodism spread to more than a half-million members by 1830, making it the leading denomination in most of the states. Today, a small Methodist congregation in Maine welcomes visitors to its charming country church.
United Methodist Church, Harrington, Maine.

From the simple wreaths placed by the entrance to the laden pine trees, everything about this quaint, snowbound church in New York's Adirondack Mountains promises a congenial, old-fashioned Christmas. *St. Anthony Church, Inlet, New York.*

soil at Jamestown, Virginia. Anglicanism was eventually established as the official religion of Virginia, first informally under the early charter of the Virginia Company, then formally under the Royal Charter of 1624. It also became the established church of the Carolinas, Georgia, Maryland, and parts of New York City.

In other areas of the colonies, the success of the Church of England was due to Thomas Bray (1656–1730). He founded an organization, the Society for the Propagation of the Gospel in Foreign Parts (SPG), which sent out missionaries, promoted the native missions, and aided the work of Trinity parish (founded 1693) in New York City. Some strong Anglican churches also sprang up in New Jersey and Pennsylvania, where SPG worked among frontier parishioners, and in New England (including the Old North Church in Boston).

THE EAST COAST

The oldest surviving church building in the original thirteen colonies is St. Luke's Church, Smithfield, Virginia, now known as Historic St. Luke's National Shrine. Begun in 1632, its architects' intent was to recreate an English church in the New World. Gothic in style, it has a steep roof, corner turrets, windows with pointed lancets, and a square tower with corner pilasters and round-arched windows on its third story. It also features a timber-trussed ceiling, no aisles, triangular pediments over the doors, and quoins (blocks of stone at the corners). Unlike most early Virginian

could be only one state religion. Nonetheless, two-thirds of the British considered themselves truly Catholic. Among the other third were the Puritans, who intended to take over the church, so they attended, and the Separatists, who did not recognized the authority of the Church of England.

In 1607, a group of Protestants—some Puritans, most Anglican—established the first permanent English settlement on American

churches, it is constructed of brick, not wood, to more closely resemble the masonry of the churches in England.

The most striking feature of Ye Olde Yellow Meetinghouse in Imlaystown, New Jersey, is the old-style pulpit, elevated about five feet, with steps on both sides. The original building was constructed about 1720; the current one was built after a fire in 1731. Extremely plain inside, it houses old-fashioned white benches with high backs trimmed in mahogany.

St. Ignatius Church, St. Thomas Manor, Chapel Point, Maryland, was originally a chapel attached to a manor house. It was erected as a private place of worship because, at the time it was built (1741), Maryland law did not permit Catholic church buildings for public worship. The present building, begun in 1789, is made of brick laid in Flemish bond, a colonial style.

Friends Meetinghouse, Flushing, Queens, was the site of the first public meeting held in New York to discuss the abolition of slavery. The orig-

inal building was extremely plain, with no floor and no heating system. The present structure was completed in 1719; the gallery was removed in 1763, and a floor installed. The building's upper story housed a school on one side; the entire building was used during the Revolutionary War as a prison, hospital, and barracks.

The city of Wilmington, Delaware, literally grew around "Old Swedes" (Holy Trinity) Church. Built in 1698 by Swedish immigrants, it is the oldest surviving Lutheran church in the United States. The steep A-frame roof was given extra support in 1750 by two arched porches which act as buttresses; the belfry was designed by Thomas Cole. Box pews and brick paving are featured inside, offset by a black wine-glass-style pulpit under an octagonal sounding board. A gallery, added in 1774, is reached by an exterior staircase. The original window glass was replaced by stained glass in the late nineteenth century. Early members of the congregation are interred inside the church, some under their own pews.

Following page:
The Shakers' simple lifestyle and superb craftsmanship are evident in the long, spindle-back pews found in the meetinghouse at Sabbathday Lake in Maine, where flowers are the only strictly decorative touch. *Shaker Meetinghouse, Sabbathday Lake Village, Maine; 1783.*

Erected by Swedish Lutherans in 1698, "Old Swedes" in Wilmington was at the heart of New Sweden, a settlement along the Delaware River that grew into modern Wilmington. It was converted to an Episcopal church in 1791. *Holy Trinity Church ("Old Swedes"), Wilmington, Delaware; 1698.*

The first Moravians to leave Saxony bound for America settled in Georgia in the early 1730s. However, on finding the colony too militaristic, members of this pacifist sect soon began moving north to Pennsylvania, where they founded the town of Bethlehem. *Historic Moravian Church, Bethlehem, Pennsylvania.*

THE QUAKERS

Quakers, members of the Religious Society of Friends, were one of the zealot groups that sprang up in England's Lake District in the seventeenth century. Inspired by George Fox (1624–1691), Quakers saw themselves as the "third way" of Christianity, emphasizing a fellowship of the Holy Spirit, as opposed to church authority or the Bible. They were given the name Quakers because they were seen trembling at the word of God during a magistrate's trial in Derby, England.

Friends believe that everyone has the potential to be a minister, so no one takes on the role of cler-

Amid the fertile Pennsylvania farmlands sits the small hamlet of Salem, home to this clapboard Gothic Revival–style Presbyterian church built in the shape of a cross. *Salem United Presbyterian Church, Salem, Pennsylvania.*

gy or laity. Their service, called a Meeting in Worship, has no ritual, agenda, or ordained minister. It takes place in a meetinghouse, unadorned by a steeple, stained-glass windows, altar, or music.

When the first Quakers, Mary Fisher and Ann Austin, arrived in Boston in July 1656, the Puritan authorities took immediate action, imprisoning them, confiscating their books, and then banishing them. However, eight more arrived two days later.

Although they were ousted from Boston, Quakers formed meetings in Rhode Island. From there they were able to gather converts from Boston, Plymouth, and other nearby areas. They were unable to expand further, however, until William Penn (1644–1718), the founder of Pennsylvania, became a Quaker in 1666, and his lands became the world's most secure home for religious tolerance. When the Pennsylvania constitution was written in 1682, it set out the terms of Penn's "Holy Experiment," allowing freedom of religion to anyone who believed in God.

Quakers eventually became the minority group in their own sanctuary when a group of dissenters was led away by George Keith. Later, the huge influx of German and Scotch-Irish immigrants further reduced the Quaker sphere of influence.

THE SHAKERS

The Quakers were the inspiration for another movement, begun by Ann Lee (1736–1784). She joined a "Shaking Quakers" group in England in 1758, which led to her seeing visions and speaking in tongues. Because of this gift "Mother Ann" began to hold her own services, which included dancing, singing, and speaking in tongues.

Ann Lee's tenets were that God and his first creatures on Earth were both female and male; Jesus Christ was the male messiah; Catholicism had failed in carrying out its mission; and that Ann Lee herself was the female messiah. Because she signaled the Second Coming she believed there

was no need to procreate, so her followers abstained from sexual relations.

In 1774, she and eight of her disciples established a Shaker group in Watervliet, New York. It was not until after her death that the first actual Shaker society was founded, in 1787, at Mount Lebanon, New York. By 1794 there were eleven communities in New York and New England; by the mid-nineteenth century, there were numerous Shaker settlements in New York, Massachusetts, Connecticut, New Hampshire, Maine, Ohio, and Kentucky. The group was officially known as the Millennial church, or the United Society of Believers. Farming was the basis of their economy, but they also developed commercial and handicraft enterprises, and became renowned for their furniture and architecture. Today a few Shakers still live at Sabbathday Lake Village in Maine.

Though the Quakers, like so many others, came to America seeking religious freedom, they were, in fact, persecuted in many of the colonies. This traditional, unadorned Quaker meetinghouse is a testament to their perseverance. *Friends Meetinghouse (Quaker), Mt. Pleasant, Ohio.*

LUTHERANS AND CALVINISTS

Martin Luther was a Roman Catholic priest with no desire to separate from the church, but he was responsible for initiating the violent eruption known as the Protestant Reformation. Luther had been taught to believe that sins were fully forgiven on earth only through faith in God through Christ, so he could not help but notice the contradictions within the church—especially the sale of "indulgences," which were said to reduce the time a person's soul spent in purgatory.

On October 13, 1517, Martin Luther posted his theories on the doors of the cathedral at the university in Wittenberg, Germany, where he taught. The result was a partial return to simpler worship and suppression of elaborate rituals and embellished vestments. Formal processions and rites gave way to plainness; the more radical reformers even set about ravaging stained-glass windows and statues. The new denomination eventually became prevalent in Saxony, Hesse, parts of southern Germany and the Baltic States, Scandinavia, Finland, and Iceland.

Lutheranism was just one of the two major branches of early Protestantism. The other branch, Calvinism—named for lawyer John Calvin and perpetuated by John Knox—held sway in parts of Germany, Geneva, Hungary, the Netherlands, and parts of France, where the Calvinist Huguenots had about eight hundred congregations. Through the Dutch West India Company, more than thirty Calvinist families settled along the Hudson and Delaware rivers in New Netherland (New York) in 1624. In 1628, a Dutch Reformed minister arrived in New Amsterdam (what was to become New York City). The Dutch continued emigrating, and by 1700 more than twenty-six churches had planted roots in New York, New Jersey, and other colonies. Later that century they were joined by immigrants from southern Germany who shared their Reformed faith. More than fifty German Reformed congregations were established, mainly in Pennsylvania, by 1740.

Knox went on to become a major force in establishing Presbyterianism in Scotland, where it is still dominant. By 1800 the movement had spread to become the most influential denomination in New York, New Jersey, and Pennsylvania.

THE MID-ATLANTIC STATES

One of the oldest and least altered Lutheran churches in the United States, Augustus Lutheran Church, is located in Trappe, Pennsylvania. It still

RIGHT: **The original St. Paul's, built in 1850, was lost in a 1918 fire. The unpretentious character of the rebuilt structure echoes the pristine beauty of the surrounding farmland and hills.** *St. Paul's Evangelical Lutheran Church, Loganton, Pennsylvania; 1919.*

OPPOSITE: **The exterior of the oldest standing Lutheran church in New England is actually quite similar to that of the Puritan meetinghouses of the day. In the cemetery rests the remains of one of the first pastors.** *German Lutheran Meetinghouse, Waldoboro, Maine; 1772.*

The simple interior of German Lutheran contains the original, square, unpainted pews and an exceptionally high pulpit. The church was built by a group of German immigrants who arrived in 1748. *German Lutheran Meetinghouse, Waldoboro, Maine; 1772.*

contains the original pews and altar (1795); two pews feature locks installed by the individuals who reserved them. In addition, elder Henry Melchoir Muhlenberg and his wife are interred under a marble slab. The building's design is similar to that of most German community churches: hewed timbers, iron hinges and latches, and a native brownstone floor.

At the time of Augustus Lutheran's establishment, several other denominations—Catholics in Maryland, Puritans in New England, and Presbyterians in New Jersey—had begun their own schools. This was the first Lutheran church to offer education; the school is said to have been used as their headquarters by George Washington's troops on September 23, 1777.

The Gloria Dei, an Evangelical Lutheran church in Philadelphia, was the first American branch of the Church of Sweden; its name was a symbol of thanks from the congregation. The site originally held a blockhouse used for defense against Native American attacks, but it was converted into a house of worship in 1677; the present structure was begun in 1697. Its tower was left unfinished until the builders were certain that a bell would be coming from their homeland.

St. Alphonsus Church in Baltimore, Maryland, built in 1842, is an example of the German Cahenslyite movement. Cahenslyitism was begun

in 1790 by the Archangel Raphael Society in Germany, and named after its secretary, Peter Cahensly. Its goal was to aid German immigrants in retaining their "Germanness," rather than surrendering to "Englishness" or Americanization. The Cahenslyites intended to remain separate, even from other Catholics, by governing their own parishes, employing German-speaking clergy, and relying on support from German and Austrian sources.

In St. Alphonsus, this movement expressed itself in English Gothic style combined with the peculiarly geometric quality of German Gothic. Designed by one of the Redemptorist Fathers (German and Austrian Catholic missionaries) who founded it, the church has a frontal tower that rises two hundred feet up to a spire made of cast iron. Inside, unlike most Gothic cathedrals, it has an open nave with no other levels.

The first Mennonite Meetinghouse in America, a log building constructed around 1683, is located in Germantown, Pennsylvania. Its first minister was William Rittenhouse, who in 1690 built the first paper mill in America. Rebuilt in 1770 of stone, then the cheapest and most hardy material, it took on simple lines suggestive of the more familiar Quaker meetinghouse. Nearby is the Church of the Brethren, or Dunkard Church. Dunkards came from Germany to Germantown in 1719; this church is the mother church of the denomination. Originally built in 1770, it was added to in 1797 and 1915.

Merion Meetinghouse, Philadelphia is somewhat different from other Friends' meetinghouses of the period. Instead of a simple rectilinear structure, it consists of a small wing attached to a larger one, forming a cross. Built by Welsh Friends in 1695, it was enlarged in 1713 to its current form.

OPPOSITE: Both John and Charles Wesley served briefly as Anglican missionaries in Georgia before returning to their home in England to found Methodism. This church is dedicated to a branch of Methodism named for the two brothers. *St. Paul's Wesleyan Church, Oxford, Maryland.*

RIGHT: **East meets west in this Orthodox church, with its impressive group of Byzantine onion domes and distinctly Colonial American facade of shingles, clapboard, and timber. Surprisingly, it is a modern building, erected in 1988.** *Elevation of the Holy Cross Orthodox Church (Parish of the Orthodox Church in America), Williamsport, Pennsylvania; 1988.*

OPPOSITE: **A tall, off-center entrance tower attached to the long side of this Presbyterian church enhances and adds "movement" to the structure's overall design, while its spire reaches to the treetops, beckoning to all.** *Tygarts Valley Presbyterian Church, Huttonsville, West Virginia.*

THE MIDWEST

As churches spread westward throughout the United States, the builders of those churches, mostly from the East, brought with them the architecture they had come to be familiar with.

The Holy Family Church in Cahokia is the oldest church building in Illinois. It was built sometime before 1833, when a small chapel was added to the front to serve as a sacristy. The church rests on a stone foundation and, although additions have been made, the original structure remains. Constructed of hewn walnut logs, it is held together by wooden pegs instead of nails, and the floor is crafted of split cottonwood.

Another notable Midwestern house of worship is St. Patrick's Church, Benton, Illinois, a stone building of random ashlar with some Gothic motifs. It was designed by Samuel Mazzuchelli, a priest who worked among the Native Americans and was the architect of several churches.

The Church of St. Joseph, Somerset, Ohio, has been called "The Shrine of Catholicity in Ohio." The original log church was built in 1818, and eventually became the priory of the Dominican religious order. Later, in 1929, it became a House of Studies and the center for much of the area's missionary work.

"The Little Brown Church in the Vale," officially the First Congregational Church of Bradford (north of Nashua, Iowa) was the subject of a 1865 musical composition by William S. Pitts. The song, "The Church in the Wildwood," invites listeners to visit the church, which is constructed of local red oak.

ABOVE: Wildflowers greet parishioners as they drive up the dirt road to Immaculate Conception, situated on the desolate grasslands of northwestern Nebraska. *Immaculate Conception Catholic Church, Sioux County, Nebraska.*

OPPOSITE: Dubbed the "Cathedral of the Plains" by William Jennings Bryan, this massive church was handbuilt of native limestone by German and Russian Catholics using ramps and blocks and tackle. It remains one of the tallest structures on the Great Plains. *Victoria, Kansas; 1909–1911.*

RIGHT: A gleaming white church acts as a beacon on the horizon of a seemingly endless stretch of land. Could this be the same scene the pioneers witnessed as they pushed further westward? *South Dakota.*

RIGHT: In 1831, a year after founding Mormonism, Joseph Smith moved his small community of followers from New York State to Kirtland, Ohio, near Cleveland. Both the land and the neighbors were so hostile, however, that they were forced to relocate to Illinois in 1839. *Mormon Temple (Church of Jesus Christ of Latter-Day Saints), Kirtland, Ohio.*

OPPOSITE: The curved, railed landing fronting Trinity Church is reminiscent of the bow of a steamboat— wholly appropriate, given the church's location on a small, picturesque island in Lake Huron. *Trinity Church, Mackinac Island, Michigan.*

RIGHT: A fanciful Victorian spire tops an otherwise simple clapboard Lutheran church on the Nebraska prairie, now a museum dedicated to preserving pioneer life. *Danish Lutheran Church, Stuhr Museum of the Prairie Pioneer, Grand Island, Nebraska; 1888.*

LEFT: Philip Johnson's modernist, non-denominational Roofless Church features a bell-shaped dome resting on granite piers. Congregants, gathered for weddings, baptisms, and other special services, are seated in chairs placed on the flagstone area around the structure. *Roofless Church, New Harmony, Indiana.*

OPPOSITE: The immensely tall spire rising from the entrance tower of this church near Grand Rapids can, on a clear day, be seen all the way from Lake Michigan. It is supported at its base by small buttresses. *Grand Rapids, Michigan.*

CHAPTER THREE

HISTORIC CHURCHES AND CHAPELS: THE SOUTH, THE SOUTHWEST, AND THE WEST

Previous page:
This simple Baptist edifice and its small, adjacent cemetery, the perfect image of a pastoral southern church, nestle in a valley in what is now the Great Smoky Mountains National Park. *Missionary Baptist Church, Townsend, Tennessee.*

RIGHT: Charleston's oldest church boasts an imposing octagonal steeple which, during the Revolutionary and Civil wars, was painted black in order to make it a less obvious target. Aside from repairs and a sacristy added in 1886, the building is still in its original form. *St. Michael's Episcopal Church, Charleston, South Carolina; 1752–61.*

A church is many things— a place of worship, a respite from daily life, a sanctuary in which to think about our sorrows, to pray, to reflect. But it is only a building. It has no life of its own; it only reflects the lives of those who worship within. The churches of America, like those around the world, were shaped by the people who came to build them. From the time of the early Catholics through the various offshoots of the Protestant faith to the present day, it was the members of the congregations who shaped the architecture and character of their churches.

SOUTHERN PROTESTANTS AND BLACK CHURCHES

Although they were segregated, slaves in the South and free blacks in the North worshipped in the same churches as whites before the Civil War. After the war, the revival movement inspired many black people to join Baptist and Methodist churches as they spread throughout the South and Southwest.

Methodism was founded in England in 1738 by an Anglican priest, John Wesley, as a movement within the existing Protestant church; it spread from England to Ireland to America. There were fifteen thousand Methodists in the United States at the end of the Revolutionary War, but all the Anglican ministers had returned to England. Wesley ordained several new ministers himself, and in 1784 the Methodist Episcopal Church in America was organized in Baltimore.

Two African denominations—African Methodist Episcopal in 1816 and African Methodist Episcopal Zion in 1821—were formed in the North; by the 1860s, great numbers of Southern blacks were joining them as well. Of the 208,000 black members of the Southern Methodist church in 1860, only 49,000 remained in 1866; in 1870 they established the Colored Methodist Episcopal church.

OPPOSITE: The South's first Baptist church was formed when its congregation moved from Maine to South Carolina in 1686. The present Greek Revival structure was designed by Robert Mills and completed in 1822. *First Baptist Church, Charleston, South Carolina; 1822.*

A rough-hewn, one-room building once served as both church and schoolhouse for the small population of southeastern Kentucky's Henley Settlement. It is now enclosed within the borders of the Cumberland Gap National Historic Monument. *Brush Mountain Church and School, Middleboro, Kentucky.*

The Baptist movement was founded by Separatist John Smyth as an offshoot of English Puritanism. He emigrated to Holland, worked for a time with the Dutch Mennonites, and in 1612 established the first Baptist congregation near London. English and Welsh immigrants, assisted by Roger Williams, organized America's first Baptist church in 1639. John Clarke, who came to be known as the most important Baptist in early America, also established a congregation in 1639, in Newport, Rhode Island; he later founded Baptist churches in Plymouth and other parts of Massachusetts. Unlike the Puritans, with whom they had common roots, the Baptists refused to let the government play any role in their church, and because of this, except in Rhode Island, they often suffered conflict.

OPPOSITE: The steeple of St. Philip's was used as a sighting range during the Civil War, and lighted at the top from 1893 to 1915 to help guide ships into the harbor. It was added in 1847 to house a gift of an eleven-bell chime and a musical clock. *St. Philip's Episcopal Church, Charleston, South Carolina; 1838.*

The Baptist movement reached blacks when "Brother Palmer" started the first Baptist church for slaves in the mid-1700s. Thousands more sprang up in the South as well as in the Northern cities. In 1895 at Atlanta, black Baptists formed the National Baptist Convention, claiming a membership of 1.8 million. Eventually, Baptists came to dominate the deep South (except for the tips of Florida, Louisiana, and Texas, where Catholicism was predominant); the Methodists moved west.

THE SOUTH

St. Augustine, Florida is home to the church of the oldest parish in the New World. The Cathedral of St. Augustine was established more than fifty years before the first permanent English settlement at Jamestown, Virginia. Two earlier churches—Nostra Señora de la Leche and Our Lady of the Angels—were dismantled and their parts sold to pay for the new building, completed by 1797 (although records date from 1594). With the exception of the limestone wall containing its

This raised pulpit with its hanging sounding board is simple and elegant, yet imposing, focusing all attention on the preacher. Its location, behind the altar, is quite unusual. *St. James Goose Creek Episcopal Church, Goose Creek, South Carolina; c. 1714.*

four "mission" bells, the entire cathedral was destroyed by fire in 1887. During reconstruction, two wings which form a cross and a tower with a gabled belfry were added.

St. James Episcopal Church in Goose Creek, South Carolina (1714) was founded by planters from Barbados who established the Church of England in the Carolinas. A colonial building near Charleston, it stands as a record of an era in which the state was a colony of Barbados, which was itself an English colony. The first truly Georgian church in the colonies, it contains a pulpit uniquely located above and behind the altar. Behind the

pulpit is a relief-molded shield of the coat of arms of George I, and a huge baroque pediment with Corinthian pilasters. The main doorway to the church features a carved pelican, native to South Carolina and used in medieval Christian iconography as a theme of the Eucharist. The nave houses box pews and a stone floor.

Many of the Charleston area's plantation churches and chapels followed the example set by St. Michael's Church, Charleston, one of the great Georgian churches of the colonies. Its focal point is a two-story Roman Doric portico, the first on any colonial Georgian church, reminiscent of that

ABOVE: Just a little way down the coast from busy Savannah, tourists and residents alike can find a moment of tranquillity in or outside of this lovely church set amid lush, tropical vegetation. *Christ Church, St. Simons Island, Georgia; 1883.*

OPPOSITE: Gravestones both old and new dot the cemetery connected to this tranquil, bucolic church in the rolling hills near the Great Smoky Mountains of North Carolina. *Asheville, North Carolina.*

ABOVE: The builders of this Presbyterian church in Florida departed from tradition with the inclusion of an entrance tower uniquely located at the corner, rather than the front, of the structure. *First Presbyterian Church, Stark, Florida.*

RIGHT: The original Christ Church, a frame structure founded in 1707, was destroyed by fire in 1725. The second church, completed in 1726, was badly damaged during both the Revolutionary and Civil wars, and restored in 1787, 1874, and 1924. *Christ Episcopal Church, Mount Pleasant, South Carolina; 1787.*

Sheldon Chapel, once an impressive, colonnaded building, has remained standing in ruins since its destruction in 1865 by Union troops. A portico with massive brick columns originally stood at the entrance, and a large, Palladian window illuminated the altar. *Sheldon Chapel Ruins (Episcopal), Gardens Corner, South Carolina; c. 1751.*

One can almost feel the ocean breeze gently blowing through the airy, sun-dappled interior of this nondenominational island chapel off the southern shores of North Carolina. *Bald Head Island Village Chapel, Bald Head Island, North Carolina.*

on Gibbs' St. Martin-in-the-Fields. The solid spire is a series of three diminishing octagons highlighted by open arches, with pilasters and cornices.

One Carolina country church that started out as part of a village—Childbury, South Carolina—has ended up as the sole survivor of the community. Strawberry Chapel is a small brick church along the Cooper River. Erected in 1725 as a chapel to Biggin Church, the parish church of St. John's Berkley, it was to be the center of a colonial town that had been completely planned, including a university. Although the chapel's two-level pulpit and balcony have been removed, murals depicting various members of the parish still line the walls.

Because of its near-perfect proportions, the wooden spire on Presbyterian Church, Savannah, Georgia, is one that is frequently studied by students of church architecture. The original church structure was also wood; it was rebuilt in 1796 and

1817, but the current white marble structure was erected in 1889. Three wide aisles split the interior of the church: The center aisle is eleven feet across, and the two side aisles more than four feet each. A flat dome and the galleries are supported by four columns.

Hands held together in prayer can sometimes be seen in the detail work of the pews of most churches across America; one hand held up, pointing toward heaven, is a gesture seen more commonly used for pulpits. In Port Gibson, Mississippi, the hand pointing toward heaven is twelve feet high, and it is not *in* the First Presbyterian Church, it is on top of it. "The Hand" (made of galvanized metal) atop the church's spire was erected as a tribute to an early minister, the Reverend Zebulon Butler, who was known for preaching with a clenched and upraised hand. This congregation's first church was erected in 1807, and the present building in 1859.

LEFT: **Bark shingles and a timber fence and columns all contribute to the delightfully rustic style of this Episcopal church, located in what is now Pisgah National Forest in the mountains of North Carolina.** *All Saints Episcopal Church, Linville, North Carolina.*

OPPOSITE: **An austere Danish Lutheran church near the shore of Lake Mattamuskeet, North Carolina's largest natural lake, discreetly draws the eye upwards to God and heaven.** *Fairfield Danish Lutheran Church, Fairfield, North Carolina.*

The impressive chancel of San Luis Rey seems to glow with an otherworldly light. The mission, built by Franciscan fathers, is the eighteenth and largest of the California chain. *Mission San Luis Rey de Francia, San Luis Rey, California; 1798.*

SPANISH MISSIONS

Although most people think of the Puritans of New England as those who first brought their European religion to the New World, the first Christian presence actually arrived earlier and much farther south. In 1543, more than one hundred and fifty Franciscan and Dominican friars went to Mexico to spread the faith. These missionaries settled to a line about two hundred miles north of Mexico City.

In 1565, Father Francisco Lopez de Mendoza Garjales, a chaplain assigned to the Spanish fleet commanded by Pedro Menendez de Aviles, established the earliest Christian place of worship in the continental United States. The chapel, called Nombre de Dios (Name of God), which was built north of St. Augustine, Florida, was the site of the first Catholic mass offered for those who came to found the nation's first permanent, non-native settlement. Shortly thereafter, the Spanish established two missions, one in Timucua, Florida in 1567, and one in Guale (in what is now Georgia) in 1569.

From 1567 to 1861, several religious denominations founded missions from coast to coast in the areas known as New Spain (Florida, New Mexico, Arizona, Texas, and California). The "mission chain" of California, built between 1769 and 1823, was the last of the large mission areas. It extended along more than five hundred miles of the old Camino Real, from San Diego to the south of Sonoma (north of San Francisco Bay).

Father Junípero Serra, a Spanish Franciscan who did not start his missionary work until the age of fifty-six, established a chain of missions along the four-hundred-mile line from San Diego to Monterey. His first mission, San Diego de Alcala, was founded in 1769, and later destroyed. The second, dedicated to San Carlos Borromeo, was founded in 1770 in Monterey; and was later moved and rededicated as San Carlos at Carmel. Father Serra died in 1784, after founding nine missions.

Somewhat naive trompe-l'oeil painting adorns the sanctuary of Mission Santa Inéz. The church was partially restored by an Alsatian priest, with the assistance of a group of homeless men, around the turn of the century. *Mission Santa Inéz Virgen y Mártir, Solvang, California; 1815–17.*

Damaged by the 1812 earthquake and suffering from much neglect, Purísima Conceptíon was eventually converted into a state park in 1935 and painstakingly restored. The belfry is quite typical of the southwestern mission style. *Mission la Purísima Conceptión, Buellton, California; 1789.*

Following page:
Typical Spanish Colonial ornamentation graces the nave of San Buenaventura, the last of nine missions founded by the famous Franciscan father, Junípero Serra. *Mission San Buenaventura, Ventura, California; 1782.*

ABOVE: Workers who built the present Santa Inéz, made primarily of brick and adobe, had to travel forty-five miles to obtain the wood for the mission's rafters. The original structure was destroyed in the 1812 earthquake. *Mission Santa Inéz Virgen y Mártir, Solvang, California; 1815–17.*

RIGHT: The first European settlement in California, Mission San Diego was founded by Junípero Serra in 1769; it was moved seven miles, to its present site, in 1775. The current structure was restored in 1931. *Mission San Diego de Alcala, San Diego, California; 1808–13.*

OPPOSITE: Native American building techniques combine with Spanish Colonial style to create this unique mission—complete with a broad plaza welcoming visitors to the church—in Taos Pueblo, New Mexico. *Mission San Geronimo, Taos, New Mexico; 1874.*

THE SOUTHWEST AND THE WEST

The Mission Church of San José de Aguayo, San Antonio, Texas, was founded in 1720 by Franciscan Father Antonio Margil and completed in the 1780s. Its famous rose window is just one of its celebrated fineries; the building is laced with beautiful carvings—cherubs, saints, pillars, facings—as well. Native American motifs are also used throughout the church's quadrangle complex, which occupies over eight acres.

The church building itself, an example of the Spanish Colonial style, is constructed not of adobe, like most mission churches, but of tufa (limestone), masonry, and stucco. Abandoned as a mission in 1803, it has been preserved since the 1930s and is now used as the local parish church.

Nine-foot-thick walls provide a more than adequate fortress at the San Estevan del Ray Mission in Acoma, New Mexico, one of America's oldest churches (begun in 1629) to survive in its original form. It has a mud floor, a fifty-foot-high roof covered with mud plaster, and two small, high rectangular windows near the altar. The altar itself is three feet high; painted canvases featuring religious images span two fifteen-foot-tall pine beams atop the altar. Outside, two square bell towers rise above the east wall, and a mud wall protects a cemetery dotted with simple headstones and

OPPOSITE: Set atop a hill, this ethereal church, made from local redwood, directs all eyes heavenward with its entrance tower and spire, steeply sloping roof, and Gothic windows and door. *St. Teresa's Church (Catholic), Bodega Bay, California; 1859.*

ABOVE: Though founded in 1786, the present Mission Santa Barbara was begun in 1815. The facade (restored in 1950), with its classical Greek details, is startlingly different from those of most of California's missions. *Mission Santa Barbara Virgen y Mártir, Santa Barbara, California; 1815–1820.*

The lovely painted interior of Hawaii's St. Benedict's Church combines traditional Christian iconography with local, tropical motifs. Columns in the narrow nave even form the "trunks" of realistic-looking "palm trees." *St. Benedict's Church, Honaunau, Hawaii.*

Once a booming gold-rush center, now a historic ghost town, Bodie, California is home to this Methodist church. A beautiful painting depicting the Ten Commandments originally hung behind the pulpit; ironically, it was stolen. *Bodie Church, Bodie State Historic Park, California; 1882.*

Early in the nineteenth century, Congregationalist missionaries from New England were the first Americans to bring the gospel to the Sandwich Islands. Their influence can still be seen in this church located on the "Big Island"—Hawaii. *St. Benedict's Church, Honaunau, Hawaii.*

The "Lourdes of the Southwest" was erected by Don Bernardo Abeyta when he touched the ground on the site and was miraculously cured of his fatal illness. Today, pilgrims still travel to the *santuario* to touch the same ground through a hole the builders made in the floor. *Santuario del Señor de Esquipula, Chimayo, New Mexico; 1813–16.*

Russian Orthodoxy remained the dominant religion of Alaska throughout the nineteenth century, well after the American purchase of the territory from Czar Alexander II in 1867. This tiny, hand-hewn log church is a charming reminder of Alaska's first white settlers. *St. Nicholas Russian Orthodox Church, Eklutna, Alaska; 1830s.*

crosses.

Fourteen of California's twenty-one early missions are still standing. One of the most architecturally interesting is Santa Barbara, founded in 1786. The mission's first church was planned by Franciscan Father Junípero Serra, but he died two years before the work began. The building was originally intended as a temporary chapel, but a permanent one was built during the 1790s; though that structure was damaged in the earthquake of 1812, another was completed by 1820.

The Santa Barbara mission is renowned for its facade, which is quite unusual among the California missions. Inside, the church features stations of the cross brought from Mexico in

1797. The designer, Padre Ripoll, was inspired by a Spanish translation of a Latin book of architecture. Today, Santa Barbara is also known for its complete mission library.

Tualatin Plains Presbyterian Church ("Old Scotch Church"), Hillsboro, Oregon, is a typical example of the board-and-batten style popular in rural America in the nineteenth century. A late example of Gothic Revival, probably based on plans from a pattern book, it is plain and vertical. Except for a hexagonal tower accented by the surrounding forest, no ornamentation stands out on the exterior of the structure. It was constructed in 1878 by several men and women from Glasgow, Scotland, and is still in use today.

ABOVE: This meticulously maintained church, located on a peninsula that juts into the Puget Sound, displays an unusual, tapered belfry between tower and spire. *Port Gamble, Washington.*

OPPOSITE: Harsh winters and blazing summers have taken their toll on this wood-shingled frontier church—sadly neglected and falling to ruin—on the high plains of Montana. *Ringling, Montana.*

INDEX

Page numbers in **bold-face** type indicate photo captions.